BENVENUTO AND GELSOMINA

A LOVE STORY

BY JACK JONATHAN AND SHEELAGH HOPE
ILLUSTRATED BY LOUIS MARAK AND LOUIE LE LAPIN

First Edition

ISBN: 978-0-9979556-0-6

MELAGRANA EDITIONS™
Verba volent, scripta manent. • *Spoken words fly away, written words remain.*

Dedicated to parents and children everywhere.

Children don't at first understand prejudice, although they will naturally respond with caution to people who are not like them. It is the influence of adults that plants the seeds of prejudice.

This story was created to stimulate our imagination to look beyond the beauty of Gelsomina and the misfortune of Benvenuto. The inner beauty of these two young people becomes far more important than their physical appearance.

Modern transportation and instant communication bring us into contact with people and cultures from the far corners of the globe. Parents who want their children to feel safe outside of their small world, will welcome the opportunity to explain to their young people the importance of distinguishing real dangers from the perceived threats of physical and cultural differences.

In a Kingdom far from here, behind the Great Mountain, at the end of a hidden valley, the King and Queen were eagerly awaiting the birth of their first child. The day had arrived and the whole castle was bustling with activity. Fresh linens were being brought to the Queen's chambers. The nursery was being prepared. The nanny was summoned from the countryside. The cook was stirring up a special broth.

Soon, the church bells sounded over the land to announce the birth of a healthy little Prince. His mother, his father, the physicians, the midwives, the nanny, and his grandmother, all pronounced him beautiful and perfect in every way.

He had ten perfect little toes. His ten tiny pink fingers looked just like the fingers of the King. His eyes were a deep golden brown, the color and shape of his mother's. He had his grandmother's smile. His nose would be a tribute to the family – straight and delicate. They named him Benvenuto, and all was well.

When his mother put her hand on the back of his head to support his little neck, she felt an unexpected bump. Everyone rushed over to have a look. What could be the problem? Then they saw it: another perfect little nose just like the first one. The Prince was born with two noses. What a tragedy! What could they do? The surgeons were summoned and asked: "Can the extra nose be removed?" After careful examination, the nose was declared an essential part of Prince Benvenuto.

IT'S A BOY!

The Chancellor was called in. Would a Prince with a defect be respected by his people?   Would a King with two noses, be able to govern? The Chancellor nodded gravely, and predicted serious problems if the loyal subjects should ever find out that their prince was not perfect. The second nose must remain a secret.

A royal tailor was called in
and asked to make a special hat to cover
the extra nose. It would have to be
so stylish that all the people in the
Kingdom would want one.

There were plain hats made by the
peasant women out of flour sacks.
There were small cute ones for children.
For the noblemen, fancy hats of silk
and velvet were designed by the best
tailors in the land.

.

It would become the new fashion.
Yes, that was what they would do.
The prince, though not perfect would be
very special! The plan worked well.
It was not long before the tailor was
very busy, making Benvenuto hats.

The women insisted on decorating
their Benvenuto hats with special lace
and embroidery. The King and Queen
were reassured that their son's secret
would never be discovered.

To make sure that Benvenuto would not be reminded of his second nose, all the mirrors in the castle had been removed. He was taught to sleep on his side. Everyone in the kingdom was instructed always to approach the Prince from the front. The King and Queen were well loved so their loyal subjects did not question these rules.

As he grew older Benvenuto found the hat annoying and he would often take it off. His nurse would rush to put it back on his head, but the boy was mischievous and would throw it off again to tease her.

Benvenuto was a handsome boy who developed a passion for learning about the world around him. The tutor was very proud of his bright, engaging student. With his many wonderful qualities, the Prince grew to be respected and loved throughout the realm.

As he approached adulthood, the noble families began to think of Benvenuto as a possible suitor for their daughters. The King and Queen knew that soon their son would be thinking about marriage. The King brought the matter up at a council meeting.

Solemnly, the King asked: "Who could our Prince marry?"

To be worthy of becoming a member of the royal family, the girl would need to be very special, not just a pretty maiden. She should be intelligent, but also wise. She should be gentle, kind, and most of all, her love for the Prince should be honest. A beautiful girl would be easy to find; but the counselors talked for hours about how to discover wisdom and sincere feelings. Finally, they agreed upon a plan and set off to search the kingdom for the Prince's bride.

No road or village in the kingdom was left unexplored. The King's counselors found many lovely maidens. Some were charming, but not very intelligent. Some seemed intelligent but were not kind. Few seemed to express honest feelings.

As they traveled throughout the country they began to despair that they would ever find a maiden worthy to be Benvenuto's bride.

One day, discouraged and tired, the counselors stopped by a little house on the edge of the woods. A tiny woman, stooping over a bucket, sat peeling apples. The delicious smell of cinnamon rose from a large kettle simmering on a fire nearby. With a twinkle in her eyes she greeted the men kindly and then, observing their tired faces, invited them to stay for a meal.

"Gelsomina," she called into the house, "We have visitors." A lovely maiden peaked playfully out of the doorway. "My Dear, please go out into the garden and pick some vegetables and herbs." "Yes, Nonna," the girl replied bending to kiss the weathered cheek. The King's counselors gasped! They had seen many beautiful girls but this one took their breath away. Gelsomina's skin had a lovely glow. Her shiny, auburn hair fell gracefully down her back.

She was slender but strong and walked with a gentle sway.
The most astonishing thing of all, however,
were her eyes. They were blue
within blue; and within that blue
they were even more blue.
And her smile!!
When she smiled it was as if
the sun had just come up.
She seemed so innocent.

With light and joyful steps Gelsomina left the little cottage and walked down a forest path toward the garden. The counselors followed her, gently questioning her about the herbs she was selecting for their meal.

She was young, only 16, and yet, she knew all the plants of the forest and what they were useful for: some made a meal more tasty, some were for healing, and some made beautiful decorations. The King's advisors were astonished at all her knowledge.

As she moved through the garden she gently chided a little rabbit who was eating a carrot. "Monsieur Lapin, you know we planted a special row of carrots for you. These are *our* carrots. You are in the wrong row." Her voice was soft and merry.

A little red bird had followed her along the rows, chirruping. She stopped a moment and offered the bird some berries. She talked to several of the animals and birds she encountered. Animals that normally would flee from people were not shy with her. She seemed to know them as friends.

The counselors concluded that Gelsomina was not only a pretty maiden, but more importantly, gentle, kind, and wise.

When they returned to the cottage, the King's advisors asked the grandmother about the girl's knowledge of plants and herbs.

"She has always been curious," the grandmother commented. "From early childhood, she has asked questions about the world around her. Her love for the plants and animals helps her to remember what I tell her about them. Now, she knows as much as I do about nature."

The Grandmother pointed to a little bookshelf in the corner beside the fireplace. The counselors walked over to it. There were books about history, philosophy, poetry and other important subjects. "Has she read all of these books?" they asked in astonishment.

"Oh yes. Her dear father read to her when she was a child. Later, when she was older, she read all of his books." The grandmother's faced flushed with pride. "She knows about the world beyond the forest and our little cottage."

The King's advisors grew more impressed. In every way Gelsomina seemed to be the girl they were looking for. But one question remained – Could she sincerely love the Prince? They whispered among themselves. It would take them longer to discover this most important quality. They decided to tell the grandmother about their quest to find a bride for Prince Benvenuto.

She was unimpressed when they proposed that Gelsomina was the ideal maiden for him. When they asked if her granddaughter could accompany them back to the palace, the grandmother was slow to reply.

Finally she agreed, on one condition: "I want Gelsomina to choose her own husband. She and the Prince need to have a chance to discover each other. If love grows up between them, they can marry."

The King's counselors were pleased with the idea. It would help them discover if Gelsomina was honest in her love for the Prince.

The grandmother took Gelsomina aside
and told her of the wonderful opportunity.
As she listened to her Nonna,
the maiden's eyes brightened
with thoughts of adventure.

An excited Gelsomina went with the
counselors to the forest near the castle.
The little cottage was beautiful and soon
she made herself at home. She planted the herbs
her Nonna gave her creating a lovely garden.
Her happy singing rang through the woods
delighting the animals.

It was the Prince's custom to ride in the forest every afternoon when the weather was fine. One spring day, as the sun kissed his face and neck, he grew hot and took off his hat and his velvet vest. Whistling softly with contentment, he let the reins go slack and his horse chose an unaccustomed path. Benvenuto sat up straight when he spotted a garden and a cottage he had not seen before.

Gelsomina, who was working in the garden, stood up when she heard the slow clip clop of the horse. She looked up at the young man with flowing black hair and golden eyes and smiled her radiant smile.

Benvenuto reigned in his horse, dismounted and bowed. Gelsomina received him graciously, unaware that he was a prince. They talked about her garden. She brought him a cup of tea prepared from herbs she had grown. They laughed for no reason, just the pure joy of sitting together in the sun, sipping tea.

The Prince soon made a habit of stopping by every day. He was impressed that this young country girl knew so much. He had been tutored by the wisest men in the land and yet, he did not know all that this maiden had learned. He was soothed by Gelsomina's gentle voice and enlivened by her twinkling deep blue eyes. He loved to watch her walk out into the garden to pick her flowers and herbs. They became more than just friends. He realized that he loved her and she loved him.

When Prince Benvenuto told his parents that he had met the girl of his dreams, they smiled. The Chancellor's plan was successful! Enthusiastically, they offered to have her over for a meal. The Prince was hesitant. How could he bring such an simple girl into the formality of the court?

"She is a very modest country girl." His voice was full of concern. "If we invite her for a meal, it has to be very informal, just the four of us around the fire. The food must be simple country food. She may not enjoy our elaborate meals."

His parents could see from his concern how much he loved the girl. His mother tried to reassure him. "We have a new cook from the countryside. I am sure she will make the kind of meal that your beloved will find delicious, Benvenuto."

The day was set for the meeting. It was a simple country supper of lentil soup, hearty bread, goat's milk cheese, and fruit.

The Prince was grateful for the simple meal. Gelsomina was delighted. "This is delicious soup. It tastes just like my Nonna's." The King and Queen smiled at each other. "Would you like to meet our new cook?" the Queen asked mysteriously. The cook was summoned from the kitchen. "Oh Nonna!" cried Gelsomina, surprised to see her beloved grandmother. They embraced joyfully and Nonna was asked to join them. She and the King and Queen were happy that Benvenuto and Gelsomina had found each other. They listened with shining faces as the young couple talked excitedly about how they had met.

That night the King and Queen spoke happily about the marriage and their hope for grandchildren. The kingdom would now be secure. But the old problem loomed again. What would they tell the girl about the Prince's other nose? When he took off his hat, she would surely see it and be alarmed. They decided to talk with the maiden the next morning. Gelsomina listened patiently. She had already seen the Prince without his hat on and was aware of the second nose. But she was puzzled. "Why are you so concerned about this?" she asked. The King and Queen told her the story about the Prince and how they had hidden his nose from the people all these years. But the girl insisted, "I love Benvenuto just as he is!" The King and Queen were still not convinced that Gelsomina's love was sincere. The next night they tiptoed into their son's room. Gently they lifted back the bedclothes and held up a candle. There, on the back of his head, was the nose. It was beautiful, but it definitely looked strange to them. Was the girl lying to them? That would not be acceptable. Or was it possible that the Prince's second nose really was not significant to her?

They again conferred with their advisors who passionately discussed their disbelief that Gelsomina seemed unaffected by the Prince's two noses. Finally, the King addressed his oldest and most trusted counselor.

"My dear friend, you have not spoken up. What is your opinion?"

The other men fell silent. What would this learned man have to add to the discussion? Respectfully, they turned to him.

The oldest counselor sensed some skepticism. But he knew what he knew and what he knew was the wisdom of the ages that is true for all people and all times.

He cleared his throat and spoke, "Your Highness, honorable gentlemen, I have listened to your wise discourse. Now, as you have asked, here is my opinion. The Prince has two noses. This is a fact. The maiden says the second nose is of no consequence to her. That is also a fact. Can these two facts be reconciled?"

In a voice that grew in strength he
continued, "It is really very simple. The
maiden truly loves the Prince
and the Prince truly loves the maiden.
When we see with the eyes of sincere love
we see only beauty. "

The room was deeply silent as each
counselor pondered this wisdom. They looked
around at each other, and with a collective sigh
of relief, they smiled. The King and Queen
embraced. Soon the room filled with sounds of
joy, as plans for the marriage ceremony were
discussed.

The wise old Counselor, with a twinkle
in his eyes, added these final words:

Let us resolve that from this day forward, our land will be known for its tolerance and respect for everyone. On the wedding day of Benvenuto and Gelsomina, let us celebrate the unique beauty that is in each of us.

Words of Wisdom
from :
Monsieur Louie le Lapin

Nature is your Friend:
Take care of it.

The best plant in our garden is an ancient apple tree.
We've been the very best of friends since I was only three.

I've eaten lots of apples in the fall when they are red.
And way up high, my tree-house sits, among her branches spread.

One summer, very hot and dry, her leaves were turning brown.
So every morning, I got up and watered her deep down.

Be True to Yourself:
Don't follow the crowd.

I have the very best of friends and we have lots of fun.
We like to go down to the park and run and run and run.

But one day at the fountain, Jake said with nasty grin,
"Hey, help me grab that little boy and then we'll push him in."

We all looked at each other, we did not want to seem
Like losers to the guy we thought was leader of our team.

This was not me; so I stepped up and faced him toe to toe.
He followed with the others when I said, "It's time to go."

Be Curious:
Explore the world through books.

At night I like to travel forth upon my Daddy's knee,
We open up a picture book and there the world we see.

The mountains reaching to the sky, a forest dark and scary,
A cloud of birds that soar way high, a polar bear so hairy.

I wonder how the stars turn on and why the lake is blue.
There are so many questions. I want to know what's true.

My Daddy says "Don't worry now, for when you're reading well,
The books will answer questions and have lots of tales to tell."

Time to Grow Up

I watch my brother running off and leaving me behind.
I wonder if I followed him, would Mommy really mind?

I think that I am big enough to go beyond the gate.
But Dad and Mom keep telling me that I must wait and wait.

Soon I'll be going off to school, I'll be away all day.
I know I'll miss my Mom and Dad, and having time to play.

Mom says that I will meet new friends and learn to read and write,
And I can snuggle up with her when I return at night.

Be Happy
With the treasures around you.

The Queen sits on her golden throne upon a velvet pillow.
I sit on a mossy bank beneath a weeping willow.

The palace food is flavored with spice from foreign lands.
My lentil soup and rustic bread are made by my own hands.

Though just a simple country girl, I'm richer than the King,
For nature shows me every day a new amazing thing.

Jack Jonathan: Author and Book Designer

Jack Jonathan is an enigma. He was born in Egypt. His mother tongue was French, but he was educated in Italian. He had a classical European education and dreamed of a career in music or college teaching. When WWII intervened he became a printer, publisher, and photographer in Cairo with the United States Information Agency.

Jack continued his innovative career with almost thirty years in new product development and marketing at Hallmark Cards and a 20-year career as President of Stowers Innovations where he wrote and published the Yes, You, Can series of books.

Jack honed his story telling skills when he made up nightly bedtime tales for his three children. For Jack, life is a fascinating saga enriched by his great sense of humor and delight in telling stories.

Sheelagh Hope: Author

Sheelagh Hope was three years old when she became aware that people liked to tell her about their lives. For thirty years as a child psychologist she listened to children and told them healing tales. Now, she delights in writing stories and poems to share with all children.

Drawing on her knowledge of human development, Sheelagh has helped write books for the Stowers Innovations' Yes, You Can series designed to help children and adults understand the value of money, enjoy a meaningful life, and become successful.

Sheelagh is called Mother by two wonderful young women. She is a story-teller on demand for her grandchildren Maya, Ally, Oliver and Hazel.

Creative Production:
Steve Barr

Lou Marak: Illustrator:

Lou Marak is one of the fortunate few who has been able to make a good living by pursuing what he loves best: creating great art. His body of work includes commercial art. His fine art has been shown in many exhibitions, principally in the Midwest and the Santa Fe area.

Lou who is very versatile, can skillfully draw humorous subjects as well as very sensitive landscapes. He is famous for his marvelous caricatures as well as his gentle portraits.

Lou is married to a well- known Kansas City artist, Philomene Bennett. Between them they have 9 children and 16 grandchildren.